THE RETIREMENT *Trilogy*

A BOOK SERIES WITH WRITTEN ADAPTATIONS FROM THE *"I'M YOUR AGENT PODCAST"*

A podcast geared towards education, information and allowing you to retire on your own terms

---

JEFFLYN *"I'm Your Agent"* **DANGERFIELD**

The information in this book is for general use. I believe the information is reliable and accurate. However, it is important to remember individual situations may be entirely different. Therefore, information should be relied upon only when coordinated with a financial professional or advisor. You should consider your specific situation including your retirement, health, and legacy goals before acting on information provided in this book. Please note that neither the information presented, or any options exposed is not to be considered as an offer to buy or purchase any insurance product referred to in this book.

The information provided should not be considered as tax or legal advice and may not be relied upon for avoiding any individual Federal, State, or Local tax obligation or penalty. Jefflyn Dangerfield is not authorized to give tax or legal advice.

- Content Analysis and Edit – Michael Hatter
- Edit And Copy Edit – PCPR and Communications
- Test Market and Review – Encore-FFS Leadership Team
- Cover Design Contribution – EGOT MS, LLC
- Formatting by Jose Pepito, Jr
- Publishing and Distribution– Lithobit Publishing, Lighting Source LLC,, IngramSpark a subsidiary of Ingram Book Publishing and Distribution
- ISBN – 978-1-63972-856-5

Copyright © 2021 by Jefflyn Dangerfield
All Rights Reserved

CONTENTS

SEGMENT 1 1
  Introduction 3
  Chapter 1 What/Who is a Retiree 7
  Chapter 2 What to do if you have a pension 10
  Chapter 3 What is a Supplemental retirement plan? 13
  Chapter 4 What to do if you are a small business owner? 17
  Chapter 5 What to do if you are Clergy or Non-Profit Personnel 20
  Chapter 6 What to do if you are an Entertainer, Athlete or Artist 25
  Chapter 7 Additional Retirement Income Sources 30
  Final Words 34

SEGMENT 2 35
  Introduction 37
  Chapter 1 401k, 403b, 457, 412b – The 400 series 41
  Chapter 2 IRA's VS Roth IRA's 52
  Chapter 3 Cash Value Life Insurance 59
  Final Words 68

SEGMENT 3 69

Introduction 71

Chapter 1 Cover Me: What you should look to cover in retirement. 75

Chapter 2 Pension Maximization 79

Chapter 3 Kai - Zen 82

Chapter 4 The Military 88

Chapter 5 It is about more than money – Legacy Building. 90

Final Words 98

DEDICATION AND THANK YOU'S

This trilogy is dedicated to my loving mother. If it had not been for all your help, kindness, generosity, and tough love when needed, I would not have made it to this point. Thank you, Mrs. Dangerfield, for making me believe I could do anything I set my mind too.

I would also like to thank The Encore-FFS Leadership Team, The EGOT MS, LLC., PCPR and Communications, and everyone who has provided input for this work. Your thoughts, encouragement, critique, and support has meant the world to me. It has been a great journey, but the ride is just beginning.

"Kudos to the author for taking a subject like retirement, which can seem overwhelming to most and breaking it into bite-sized bits of knowledge for the masses to understand!"

Javier Rodriquez,
Executive Field Chairman,
First Financial Security

**BOOK 1
SEGMENT 1**

THE RETIREMENT TRILOGY:

A BOOK SERIES WITH WRITTEN ADAPTATIONS FROM THE "I'M YOUR AGENT PODCAST"

A podcast geared towards education, information and allowing you to retire on your own terms

---

INTRODUCTION

It has been several years since I took pen to hand (laptop to knee) to share. The timing, for these words, is for such a time as this. The format of the book works well for this kind of information because a series of guides can be shared to help all of us become better people.

We should all be able to read 25 pages without getting bored or overwhelm. That right! Just 25 pages of information including pictures and antidotes. This book (the first of three) will feature exerts from the podcast "I'm Your Agent" a podcast geared towards information, education, and helping people choose to retire on their terms.

When most people under 30 think of retirement they often think of old people and old things. However, when you reach 40, for most retirement becomes a very real and important consideration. The realization of not working for the rest of one's life becomes very realistic. And more than that, the realization of possibly not having money to live on, becomes a very vivid thought.

Money helps to guarantee lifestyle and health so, yes this is an important topic to discuss. With 50 considered the new 30, and 60 being the new 40, what once seemed old is no longer. With the new tech generation and social media lifestyle for information gathering and transfer, things become old in less than 24 hours. However, when it comes to financial planning for this season of one's life, most think we have more time than we do. A new year always has 365 days, but it seems to come sooner with each year of age.

The goal of this series is to help both those who are considering their options and those who may not have made retirement a priority, look to a comfortable and exciting lifestyle that offers a wonderful future by providing practical tips and necessary information.

SEGMENT 1
TABLE OF CONTENT

Chapter 1 Who/What is a Retiree

Chapter 2 What to do if you have a pension.

Chapter 3 What to do if you have an alternate or supplemental retirement plan.

Chapter 4 What to do if you are a Small Business Owner.

Chapter 5 What to do if you are Clergy or Non-Profit Personnel

Chapter 6 What to do if you are an Entertainer, Athlete or Artist

Chapter 7 Additional Retirement Income Sources

Chapter 8 Final Words for Segment 1

CHAPTER 1

WHAT/WHO IS A RETIREE

Okay, this chapter is for all of you who woke up thinking you were 25 then looked in the mirror and realized that was 25 years ago even though you still look good. It is also a wake-up call for all of you who woke up at 25, in your parents' home, with a brand-new career and your first 401k plan, thinking it will last forever….

You may want to think of a retiree like changing or replacing the tires on a vehicle. The vehicle is you… yes, you are the car of your dreams. The care for your car will cost you more money as it ages than you would spend when the vehicle is new. In this illustration, your tires, and your engine (your health and lifestyle) are the most important parts of the vehicle. Your dollars are the fuel, and your tires are the tools that you use to help your engine run properly on the road for the rest of your life. Your tires also make sure that you can keep driving safely, in all types of weather and through all types of terrain.

Merriam -Webster says that a Retiree is a person who has retired from a working or professional career (a vintage or older model car driven for enjoyment, entertainment, and showmanship). If you notice it does not say what age this person should be when this is done. Traditionally, when you think of retirement, you think of a person that is age 60 or older. Some professions state that a person cannot retire from their employ until they are 65. Others provide a minimum age requirement of 55 with an additional requirement of 30 years of service on the job.

Some others state age 50 is the magic number with a minimum of 20 to 25 years worked. Just remember to be a vintage vehicle you must have gotten it when you were old enough to drive it (age 16-20), received the education and experience to drive it (age 18-25), and owned and maintained it for at least 20 years (age 40 plus). Also, remember the better you take care of your vehicle the more valuable it becomes.

Finally remember, even though you may not use it as much you still need to drive it, so it operates properly. The same with retirement.

This definition identifies there is no set age to become a retiree. But what it also identifies is that the person who states they are a retiree must have retired (concluded employment with an employer, withdrawn from one's position/occupation, or concluded one's working career). This means you must have worked to retire.

Sorry, inheriting or gifting does not qualify as a form of retirement income. However, inheritance and gift income can be used to live on at retirement.

What also is implied by the word retiree is that a certain amount of income has been generated during the career. It does not state that the person leaving employment will have an income when they leave their job (you work to have money to put fuel in your car today while you are working, but you may not have saved money for fuel in the future).

To ensure you will have an income in the future you would have to have a plan in place that makes that happen. That plan can include a pension or defined benefit, a 401k, a 457, a 403b, a 412, a social security benefit, a second job or career, an inheritance, savings accounts, stocks, bonds, mutual funds.... you get my drift.... or any combination of these plans. It should be your hope that your plan or income is enough to maintain your lifestyle once your employment or career has concluded. The following chapters will discuss some of those plans and how they affect the retiree's income.

CHAPTER 2

WHAT TO DO IF YOU HAVE A PENSION

Some retirees leave their employment or career with what is called a pension. This begs the question what is a pension? A pension is a fixed sum of money paid regularly to a person when they leave their job or career (an ongoing resource to put fuel in your car). Pensions are also known as defined benefit plans. CNN Online states that only 4% of American Employers offer defined benefit plans. This 4% may include Governmental agencies, school districts, some medical professionals, law enforcement agencies, some airlines, and some other privately-owned companies. The 4% is down from 60% in 1980. As you can see, pensions are slowly but surely disappearing.

The company that issues the pension may have contributed 100% or a portion to the fixed sum. The employee or career personnel looking to retire may also have contributed a portion to the fixed sum. However, the fixed amount is generally 40% to 70% of the former employee's salary.

Something to remember: a pension is never meant to supplement 100% of the person's income.

The difference between the benefit amount provided and what may be needed to maintain the retiree's lifestyle is called a gap. Simply put the difference between what you get from your employer and what you need to live on is your "gap". Quick example - Your employer pension gives you $4,000, you need $6,000 to live, your gap is $2,000. Please let that soak in… Most people who retire with a pension will have a gap. (Most pensions will not give you all the money you need to fuel your car and the rest of its maintenance for the rest of your life.

Most pension providers set up their pension funds with this thought in mind at retirement, retirees should have less expense. They should not need as much money to live on during retirement as they did before they retired. That may or may not be true.

Defined benefit plans do not account for any increase in taxation. Although most companies may provide what is called a "Cost of Living Allocation" (COLA) to help meet rising costs (inflation), COLA's do not meet the current inflation rate so the expenses of the retiree can still be much more than the income received. Here is an example of this: I work with a person whose mother retired over 20 years ago with an income surplus (the amount she had left after paying her bills) was $1,500.

Over time and with rising cost, considering that everything doubles in price every 18 years due to inflation, she now does not have enough money to cover the same expenses that she had when she retired even though she still receives a COLA increase every year.

So how do you bridge the gap? You may want to set up a supplemental retirement plan to offset the difference.

Something else to consider. A 401k, 403b, 457, or 412 plan, is not a pension (defined benefit). These plans are supplemental plans (voluntary contributions). Chapter 3 will provide more regarding these plans.

CHAPTER 3

WHAT IS A SUPPLEMENTAL RETIREMENT PLAN?

Simply put, a supplemental retirement plan is a plan you voluntarily set up for yourself (you set aside money of your own on your own to fuel your car). Between 1968 and 1978 the Internal Revenue Service (IRS) created the 401k, 403b, 457, and 412 codes. In 1980 it became popular for the IRS to allow employers to utilize these codes to create what is now known as retirement benefit plans for their employees. The codes were intended to allow taxpayers a break on taxes on deferred income – advanced income without paying tax on it.

During that time there were more than 20 tax brackets. Meaning if you deferred paying your taxes on that income, you were more than likely put into a lower income bracket which should (operative word should) cause you to pay less tax. Currently, there are only 6 tax brackets, so you are more than likely to stay in the same income bracket even if you defer your income.

That more than likely means less tax brackets may not provide tax savings for deferred income.

When first started the employer and the employee both contributed funds to these accounts. Currently, for these plans, the employee contributes a percentage or a set amount from their salary. The employer may or may not contribute a percentage. The employer contribution is called a match. The match can range from a percentage of the employee's salary to a dollar-for-dollar contribution of the entire salary. The employer chooses the match amount. In today's market, it is generally 3% to 5%. The match is a good thing. It is money that your employer gives you to help you put fuel in your gas tank.

Many employers have adopted these plans in place of or in addition to pensions. They do this to receive the tax advantages for their company and to the proposed employees. Additionally, most companies may allow employees to opt out of these types of plans if they choose. However, some companies mandate their employees to participate.

One thing that rings true in these and traditional pension plans is that they were never meant to provide 100% of the employee's salary at retirement. As stated in the last chapter they were only meant to absorb 40 to 70 percent.

Additionally, these types of plans are market-based – invested in the stock market (The Wall Street Roller Coaster). That means that 100% of the contribution in the employee's account is subject to stock market gains and risks (ups and downs). That is why, depending on when a person retires, they may lose money in their retirement account. Here is an example to consider: You are 40, you want to retire when you are 60. You have a 401k. Six months before you retire the market is up and you have 400k in your account. The next quarter when you get your statement it shows you only have 300k in your account. You lost money due to the market being down for three months and you have no way to make it back. The 100k that you lost will change the amount you have to live on.

The hope for all people in these types of investments is that the opposite will happen. That the market will go up or at least stay the same before they retire but that is the risk of these types of accounts.

This does not happen with a defined benefit. There is a caveat to that statement. The total pension fund (funds from everyone that contributes and the employer contributions) is subject to market risks which may cause the entire fund to be exhausted if the market hits a bad downturn. That means the person who owns and/or administers the pension dollars to its participants may run out of money to pay their employees. In other words, there may not be enough money in the fund to continue paying benefits. However, by definition, defined benefits are set up to pay the employee for the rest of their lives. It is also the job of the people investing the benefit funds to vet the investments for their safety and risk to their employees.

So how do you bridge the gap between the amount contributed to the fund, the potential amount that may be lost due to market risks, and the salary the employee was accustomed to? It is the employee's (your) responsibility to set up a supplemental plan to fill the gap.

Grandma said it like this…. always put something away for a rainy day. Nobody is gonna take care of you but you!

CHAPTER 4

WHAT TO DO IF YOU ARE A SMALL BUSINESS OWNER?

Most small businesses take years to be successful. Despite the overnight successes like Facebook, it takes most of them 2-3 years to be profitable and 7 to 10 years to say I have arrived. This is after the business plan, the small business loan, the sweat equity, and everything else that goes into making a business run. One of the biggest downfalls of small businesses is planning for all elements of success. Succession planning and or retirement planning is one of those elements. The small business owner is so busy trying to make the business go, they do not see what happens after that in their rearview at all.

As a small business owner, you are responsible for all retirement funding for yourself. Additionally, if you have partners, employees, assets, the key members of the business and the business assets should be outlined. All assets should be itemized and protected instead of separation or changes. You should also have strategies to protect key personnel individually. This protects the business owner in place of attrition or replacement. Finally, you should consider what will happen if the business is dissolved or sold.

"The need to offer holistic and personalized benefit options that offer employees the financial protection they need during the unexpected moments in life have never been greater (Kimberly Dustin, Columbus Life, California Broker November 2020)".

If you choose to offer retirement benefit options to your employees that may be a plus for your business. Offering employees benefits helps the employer to retain and attract quality employees, increase employee productivity, increase employee satisfaction, control health and welfare costs and help employees make better financial decisions (MetLife study from psi online). Additionally, offering incentives and bonuses for high-level performers is a great way to set your business apart from other companies. (You are the man/woman – high five- smiley face emoji- big ups!)

With the biggest challenge right now for many small businesses being simply to stay afloat, the last thing a small business owner wants to worry about is the nuts and bolts of keeping their employees covered. These benefits should be allocated in the business plan from day one and budgeted as a monthly, quarterly, or annual expense the same way other office or administrative expenses are budgeted. These core things are not as "nice too" if

I have a little left over or when I become profitable. They should be viewed as necessities for developing and maintaining a solid business.

Small business owners have options regarding how to set up plans for their employees. They can choose to pay for none, some, or all the benefits offered. The key is setting yourself apart by offering them. Supplemental plans like 401k's may offer tax benefits to the business and the employees. However, other options may be more cost-effective and provide the same or similar support. Seeking financial advice from a qualified financial advisor will help you make the best-informed decision for you and your business.

CHAPTER 5

WHAT TO DO IF YOU ARE CLERGY OR NON-PROFIT PERSONNEL

Clergy and Non-Profit organizations are a special breed. They are often overlooked when it comes to retirement planning. In the traditional sense, faith-based employees like Ministers, and Clergy Staff often view their work as a service. They offer those services for little or no compensation. Especially in smaller church platforms (100 members or less), Ministers, Pastors, and other Clergy serve tireless hours with minimal compensation or support.

Most often the administrative staff of the church has not been educated to the level of business that allows them to offer a retirement plan or succession plan for their ministry staff. They are "mom and pop" shops and most treat them as such.

Quite frankly, like many small businesses they are "robbing Peter to pay Paul" to keep things running. These organizations generally depend on the tithes and offerings of the church membership to survive. Those fortunate enough to have outside sources of income (i.e., rental income, daycare service income, grant funding, outside donations, etc.) generally have more leverage when it comes to financial options. But most are barely surviving. The congregation often looks to the Pastor or leadership to foot the bills for the ministry. (That is one reason for the building fund, the special offering, the 20, 50, 100-dollar lines).

If the Pastor and ministry staff should receive a stipend or salary, often the congregation looks to them to forgo or reinvest these monies into the church life's breath. That is why, despite public opinion, there are some Pastors and their families who are living a lifestyle much less than they should be at retirement age (with your best charismatic whoop…. can I get a witness)?

An additional caveat is that many are still under the old school way of thinking "people should not get paid to serve God. Your service or ministry gift should be a donation." This biblical debate goes as far back as the beginning of time. But the truth that no one can dispute is it will take money to live in this world even if we/he/they are not of this world. Retirement planning is a necessary thing for Clergy just like any other person. And just like anyone else, the sooner you begin to plan the better it is for all concerned.

That brings me to a real-life experience. Before COVID-19, for many years like many others, I was a strong churchgoer. I have seen this play out several times over. Let me share one example with you. I was a member of a church where the church property was bought by the city for a rezoning and rebuilding project. Due to the loss of membership, the church's income (tithes and offerings were down). Also, to supplement part of the expense the church was renting their building to another smaller congregation on off-hours. The church did give the Pastor a small stipend which often was redeposited to cover expenses.

The leadership of this church was paid a large sum for the sale of the property. It was stated in the contract of sale that the money received would be used to purchase a new property for the church, improvements if necessary, and church expenses. The contract did not state where the property had to be purchased but it did state all funds were to be used for the purchase of property and the benefit of the ministry. The church secretary which had been in that position since the church was organized over 40 years ago took pride in being the controller over the funds. After more than a year of searching for a church, the property was purchased and there was a surplus left for improvements and church staff. To date, the Pastor of the church is working more than 40 hours per week on a secular job which pays his living expense. His retirement plan includes a 401k from his employer and an Indexed Universal Life Policy which he set up on his own. To date the church congregation has not established any type of succession plan for the pastor, his family, a new pastor should one be needed, or the staff. The mindset is that of 40 years ago. If the church needs, the Pastor can contribute towards its needs, but the church should not have to pay/support the Pastor in retirement. He is a servant and should donate his service as such.

Now, let's be clear and fair. That is not always the case. Some in this new generation see the church as a true business and not a kitchen table operation. Even though the saving of souls and lifting of spirits is the core of its business, this new generation realizes that it will take money to support the staff and team that assists with the work. They are more open to having the church support itself, its staff, and its community. Using biblical principles, these forward thinkers are more open to having multiple streams of income to meet their financial obligations which include taking care of their key employees and sub-contractors. They understand the necessity of retirement and succession planning. I am still looking forward to the day when the right balance of the "business of ministry" and "the ministry of business" is reached.

It is time to talk about Non-Profit Organizations (the church can be a part of this group also). Smaller non-profit organizations have a similar challenge in that they have little funding and financial support. Several of these organizations do not have any type of plan in place for retirement. If grant-funded, their grant may include a succession plan, but often this is not the case. Others may have small retirement benefit plans (normally 401k or 403b plans) but traditionally they will only supplement 30 to 50 percent of the employee's salary. Not only are the salaries traditionally low, but the benefit packages also if offered are exceptionally low in comparison. If the individual does not set up an additional plan for themselves outside of what their organization offers, the person or staff member **will not have enough income to maintain their lifestyle at retirement.**

This outcome is devastating but it can be overcome.

Establishing retirement plans for Clergy and non-profit organizations is an easy thing to do. There are varied options to choose from when considering these plans. They can be set up for individuals as well as groups. However, a qualified financial advisor is necessary to assist in the process as all retirement plans may not be allowed for these groups.

As an additional benefit, some financial advisors can also set up plans that offer additional donations to the church or non-profit organization. This provides a win-win for all parties concerned.

CHAPTER 6

WHAT TO DO IF YOU ARE AN ENTERTAINER, ATHLETE OR ARTIST

Entertainers, Athletes, and artists are also a unique group. This group is challenged with transforming lives and providing escapes. Giving hope and opportunity to people of all walks of life. Opposite of Clergy, and non-profit organization, they generally make lots of money in a small amount of time. This money also comes with high taxes. The challenge becomes not to spend it all, putting enough away for "Uncle Sam" and future years. The other challenge is not to get a God complex while climbing the ladder to success. Challenge is the operative word. It is easy to spend as much or more than you make. It is even easier to spend it before you get it.

In a previous life (before becoming a retirement strategist) I worked in the entertainment industry. Although it is made to look easy, it is hard work (that is why it is called "Show" business). It requires discipline that most do not possess and are not willing to acquire. I authored a book entitled Artist Development from a Godly point of View. It is a pocket-size guide on how to be good at the Show and the Business. After more than a decade of experience and climate change in the industry, I took another direction that landed me here, but I will never forget that experience.

Most people who are successful in entertainment generally have a career span of 5 to 10 years. During that time, there is generally a team of people that advise them on how to spend their dollars. Some good, some not so good. No matter how large or small, the team generally gets paid before the person. Often these advisors pick great investments for the now. However, few of them talk about maintaining an income for the future. It is a fast-money, ego-driven life which suggests making as much as you can now because you do not know how long it (the money), or your career will last. Practical lifestyles go out the window quickly when dollars begin to flow.

This career breeds on lavish lifestyles which require lots of money to be spent on appearance and profile "The Show". Drugs, booze, women, men, parties, trips, planes, cars, clothes, and any other thing you can think of can and will consume finances if not managed appropriately. Additionally, retirement strategy is rarely discussed as retirement is generally not a priority. The mindset is set toward the now, the moment, not the future (microwave on steroids). Overnight successes that have worked years and years for that one night to come, never think that the night may end. Unless surrounded by a grounded and influential support system, tomorrow is not an option. The only thing that matters is the individual's current five minutes of fame, success, and glory.

Most entertainment and athletic contracts do indemnify (protect) the companies that issue them, to their high-performing talent. These insurance policies ensure that the company is not liable for any personal debt the client may have incurred. If needed, these policies payout to the family or the person after all expenses and advances are recouped. Here is an example. The contract is 1mil, the expenses to support the contract are 1.5mil. The client is now in debt of 500k before receiving a dime.

Some companies also offer pensions to high-profile candidates that cover lifetime income and/or health benefits. However, most entering these fields' careers do not last long enough to receive the defined benefit options provided.

The second challenge with this breed is endorsements, guest appearances, speaking engagements, and other businesses. These are alternate streams of income with high tax implementations attached. High money earners generally have large investments like homes, boats, stocks, coins, precious metals, trading cards, etc., however, if you notice retirement planning is not in that group. If successful, these ventures generally yield expansive brands, high profile, and high tax bills for the clients. Many clients mismanage these efforts by trusting friends and family who are not financial professionals, to help them with these concerns. Others may trust advisors provided or referred by the companies they have signed their contracts with who should but may not have their best interests at heart. This may cause more problems than benefits.

The third challenge with this group is once their glory days have ended most are still incredibly young. A second career should be planned early on. However, most do not think that the first career will fade, so no plans are in place. Due to the lack of planning, most of the money earned has been spent or mismanaged leaving them without funds to retire. Big homes, fancy cars, lavish jewelry, overrated parties, and much more may be seized or repossessed with nothing left to show for all the hard work it took to get them. I do not have to remind you of the published stories about artists and bankruptcies (TMZ, TV One, VH1, and YouTube tell you everything you need to know¬), or performers on skid row or driving Uber or Lyft.

Athletes, Entertainers, and recording artists should consider setting up supplemental plans for themselves early on (from check number one not just the big one). Remember everyone is not going to get the big shoe deal, open a restaurant, join a gaming team, set up a clothing or makeup line, or become a sportscaster. Most will be telling that one story where "I opened for……fill in the blank, or I played with …… in High school.

Setting something aside from check one will help these talented individuals to support themselves and their families if they should become injured, ill, or can no longer perform. The younger they are when they begin the planning process for the exit of the game, the better it is for all involved. Financial professionals in the field of retirement that can work in direct contact with agents, business managers, and or family members are the best option to ensure future income plans are successfully implemented.

CHAPTER 7

ADDITIONAL RETIREMENT INCOME SOURCES

There are two additional income sources that you can currently look forward to, to help you in retirement. The first source is Social Society (SSI/SSA). Wikipedia lets us know this about the history of SSI in the United States: "A limited form of the Social Security program began as a measure to implement "social insurance" during the Great Depression of the 1930s when poverty rates among senior citizens exceeded 50 percent. The Social Security Act was enacted on August 14, 1935. The Act was drafted during President Franklin D. Roosevelt's (FDR) first term by the President's Committee on Economic Security, under Frances Perkins."

Although there have been amendments and addendums added to the original act. The core of the plan has stayed the same. Let's look at what was created. FDR created this vehicle to help seniors during and after the great depression. But the problem with this great encounter was you could not receive a payout until age 65. The life expectancy of men was 58 and women was 62.

So, FDR never really expected anyone to receive any financial benefit. Now here is the funny thing (ironic not ha-ha) two years after the act was in place the unexpected happened. In 1937 Ernest Ackerman received the first lump-sum payout (of 17 cents) in January. So, game on. And from then until now payments have been made to Seniors from the United States Government, in hopes of supplementing their income. Some 85 years later with slips, slides, age increases, income increases, and people living longer, Social Security is still in place.

Here is something else to consider when it comes to SSI, no matter what the payout was, the country was coming out of a depression. Inflation was almost non-existent. The barter system was in full force. That made any additional funds received from the government enough to live off until the transition from this earth. Or at least that was the expectation. Not the case now. Although some people look to SSI to take care of their financial needs at retirement, it may not be enough. Additionally, government regulators and lawmakers may make it more difficult for funding to be allocated to this source. Budget cuts and the increasing senior population causes us to believe that there is no guarantee SSI will be in existence when many looking to retire reach qualifying retirement age.

The second government allocation that assists with income at retirement is Medicare or Medical for low-income families. This is the government's medical coverage supplement for most Seniors who were born and or have worked in the United States. Medicare pays for 80% of Hospitalization and Doctor's Visits. Medical may pay 100% but it can only be received if you are considered low income generating $24,000 annually or less. Nevertheless. Medicare/Medical is put in place to help seniors pay for the high cost of medical care for the aging.

People receiving pensions (defined benefits) from other sources may have their SSAE distribution decreased or eliminated due to the Windfall Act. Yes, The Windfall Elimination Provision (WEP) is a statutory provision in the United States law that affects benefits paid by the Social Security Administration under Title II of the Social Security Act. It reduces the Primary Insurance Amount (PIA) of a person's Retirement Insurance Benefits (RIB) or Disability Insurance Benefits (DIB) when that person is eligible or entitled to a pension base. (Wikipedia). So even if you paid into social security and have enough quarters to qualify for distribution, your pension income may cause you not to receive any additional money from SSI at all. If for no other reason this should cause you to want to get accurate information regarding these sources, you should seek professional support.

Final Words

Key things to take away from these pages.

- ⇨ This is a mini resource. For more in-depth information check out the podcast "I'm your Agent" at https://podcasts.apple.com/us/podcast/imyouragentpodcast/id1531948189 and seek a financial professional to assist with setting up a retirement or retirement supplemental plan.
- ⇨ Set a goal for what it will take to maintain your lifestyle once you retire, or your career is over.
- ⇨ Start your supplemental plan as soon as possible. The younger you begin to save the less you may have to save to secure your retirement goal.
- ⇨ Be aware that if you work or secure income from a professional career you will have an income gap that will need to be filled.
- ⇨ Remember to factor paying taxes into your plan.
- ⇨ If you are in entertainment, a professional athlete, or an artist, make sure that you set aside a percentage of every check you receive from every source you receive towards a future retirement plan.
- ⇨ If you are a small business owner, the sole responsibility for retirement planning for yourself and the business is on you. The cost, however, may be shared.
- ⇨ Expect to have more than one stream of income coming to you to maintain your lifestyle.

The next segment of the book in this series will take a deeper dive into the different types of retirement plans, who offers them, and how you can maximize them to generate the most income. Look forward to receiving more information, education, and material on how to help you retire on your terms.

**BOOK 1
SEGMENT 2**

THE RETIREMENT TRILOGY:

A BOOK SERIES WITH WRITTEN ADAPTATIONS FROM THE "I'M YOUR AGENT PODCAST"

A podcast geared towards education, information and allowing you to retire on your own terms

INTRODUCTION

Almost every other day you can find a new article about 401k plans. Additionally, government employees plan such as 403b's and 457's also have high exposure. Millions are exploring their options, setting up new plans, and exploring the benefits of these types of retirement alternatives. During tax season the topic of retirement plans always becomes more prevalent as CPAs and Tax Preparers review the benefits of these account contributions to lower taxable income and other potential write-offs. The funny thing about this is, year after year many candidates still have no clue what they have gotten themselves into and how to get out of it if necessary.

This segment in the book will take a deeper dive into 401k, 403b, and 457 plans (the 400 series). It will also share some tips on "Tax-Free" options such as Roth IRA's, Roth 403b's, and some cash value life insurance products that may provide great benefit at retirement.

So, strap in and get ready for the ride….

SEGMENT 2
TABLE OF CONTENT

Chapter 1   401k, 403b, 457, 412b

Chapter 2

- Traditional IRA vs ROTH IRA
- ROTH Conversion
- Things Women Should know at Retirement.

Chapter 3   Cash Value Life Insurance

CHAPTER 1

401K, 403B, 457, 412B – THE 400 SERIES

This is how most of us can feel when the IRS begins to throw out numbers and codes to us. Whether starting a new job, changing a career, or retiring at some point, you will hear 401k, 403b, 457, or 412b. So, let us begin with a point of clarity. Technically a 401k, 403b, 457, or 412b (lovingly referred to as the 400 series in the future) is an IRS code not a retirement or savings plan. It is the number the IRS uses to identify what type of contribution, what entity, what specific contributions, and what age limits can be utilized by employers and financial professionals when entering these types of contracts used for retirement.

The 401k was first introduced in the United States in the Revenue Act of 1978, amending the Internal Revenue Code. It started gaining wider adoption in November of 1981 when the IRS proposed regulations clarifying valid sources of income for 401 (k) contributions (cnbc.com). The other codes were adapted later. Each code has different but similar regulations that mandate how they can be applied. Additionally, these plan codes were initially established as a supplement for defined benefit plans and/or social security (that means pensions in laymen's terms). The 400 series were never meant to take care of 100% of retirement. Like defined benefit plans and/or social security they are only set up to take care of 30% to 70% of your retirement income. The original thinking behind these plans was to aid the 3-legged stool shared by most financial planners. So, what is that…. The "three-legged stool" is an old phrase that many financial planners once used to describe the three most common sources of retirement income: Social Security, employee pensions, and personal savings. It was expected that this trio would together provide a solid financial foundation for the senior years. None of the three was expected to support most retirees on its own. And since the 400 series was set up to take the place of most defined benefits. All three legs are still necessary to ensure you are covered during that time. (Investopedia.com)

Your parents' three-legged stool for retirement

The 400 series are a special type of investment account in which you deposit and accumulate money for use during retirement.

Many financial professionals suggest these types of accounts for savings for several reasons which include:

1. The funds are deducted from your paycheck before you get it. This helps several of us who have spending challenges. The money is taken before it gets to your hands, so the presumption is, they help you save.
2. Generally, when this money is taken from your paycheck by your employer it is considered taxed deferred meaning the taxes on this money will be paid when the money is withdrawn or utilized. This is called a pre-tax deduction.
3. Because the money is deducted pre-tax, the amount of your check which is taxed is lessened by the amount contributed to the retirement plan. This lessens the amount of income that you must report to the IRS in the current year by the amount that is put into the plan. Potentially lowering the taxable amount of income, you must report and possibly changing your tax bracket. This could change the amount of taxes you have to pay or the refund you receive in your favor. The IRS sets limits on how much can be contributed towards these accounts each year. In this year, 2021, for example, it is $19,500 with and a catch-up provision (in layman's terms "a way to add more money") when you turn age 50, which pushes that amount to $26,000.

In his article "Why 401k's are better than Pension Plans", financial enthusiast Dave Ramsey posted this chart to highlight the benefit of the 400 Series Accounts.

401(k) vs. Pension: What's the Difference?

	401(k)	Pension Plan
What's the average rate of return?	12% or more	~7%
What happens to the money when I die?	Passed down to your heirs	Dies with you or sent to your spouse at a lower amount
Who owns the account?	Employee owned	Company owned
How long do the checks last?	Until the money is gone	Your lifetime
Do I have a say in the investments?	Yes	No
Can the money be moved to another account?	Yes	Not often

The only challenge with this information is the proposed rate of returns. They are subject to change based on the type of vehicle your dollars are invested in but overall, the 400 series seems like a great "win-win" situation for you, the employer, and the IRS.

Here are some challenges that the 400 series present.

1. When these codes were implemented, there were 30+ tax brackets. Today there are only 7. (See Appendix 1 and 2 for verification). Today the probability of changing your tax bracket is unlikely.

2. Historically, taxes have risen over time, so when accessing 4 series money, you may have to pay tax at a higher rate than when you put the money into the account. This will cause you to have less money than you expected when you start utilizing these funds.
3. In addition to higher taxes, high inflation generally follows. Simply put "you pay more and get less". On average every 18 years prices double. So, if you live more than 20 years after you retire, you can expect to pay twice as much for an item than you did before you retired. Here is an example the average cost for a loaf of bread was $1.30 to $1.60 in 1999, today the same loaf of bread ranges between $2.54 and $3.65 (costaide.com). In short, even if you max out your contributions with the added amounts for bonus years at age 50, the amount you accumulate may not be enough to maintain your lifestyle when you need it. Not good if you like comfort.

Let me give you a real-life example of what I am talking about. One of my colleagues had a client that had a 401k. When they retired at age 65, they had well over $300,000 in their retirement fund. They could receive Social Security and do, and they had some money in savings. They were sure they were covered. They said when asked about setting up an additional supplement retirement plan, most of us advisors hear often, "I'm good". A familiar response by many. This was back in the '80s. This client was sure their $300,000 + their SSI, + their savings would = enough and would see them through their retirement years. They began to draw money from their account. After 15 years their $300,000 + was almost gone. At age 80 they had to reenter the workforce on a part-time basis just to generate enough money to live every day. Even as I write this, I sit "SMH" (shaking my head) because so many people find themselves in this situation. This is because they think "I'm good." The lack of planning, consulting a professional, overspending, and not accounting for inflation plus the rise in taxes will get you every time.

Here is something else you need to know about the 400 series. They are generally based in the stock market. The rule with the stock market is the same rule that governs gravity. What goes up must come down. No matter what your risk tolerance may be (conservative, moderate, or aggressive) you have no guarantees. That is why most financial experts compare the stock market to a roller-coaster going up a down. Even though the reset button has been estimated to ensue every 10 to 12 years, no one knows when there will be a change in the market.

So how does that affect your retirement?

Since you do not know where the market will be when you retire you do not know whether the market and your funds will be up or down when you need them. That is one reason why savvy financial professionals suggest a mix of investments during your savings period. Some suggest that the longer you must invest, the more aggressive you can be, however as you get closer to retirement "safe money investments" may be more attractive. Let us look at some facts that support this possibility. As you could see in the graph if you started investing in 1996 and stated to withdraw after 2016 any losses that you may have incurred, you would have had time to make that money back and start gaining money again. But what if you did not have time to regain or restart your savings process? What if there was a way to never lose any money and always start from a point of gain? Would that be better for you at retirement? Something to consider. Ok, let us get back to the 400 series.

If you have one of The 400 series, you have 3 options to access your money when you retire:

1. Leave it with your current employer and withdraw as desired - If your current employer allows the funds to stay with them, you have the option to leave the money there. However, remember the majority of 400 series accounts are market-based (placed in the stock market to earn additional funds) and are subject to the risk of the market during the time the funds are there. If the market goes down, your retirement funds will go down possibly leaving you with less money to withdraw when needed. Also, consider what may happen if your employer goes belly up, you potentially lose your money.

2. Roll it over to an IRA – Individual Retirement Account – Some employers require that you take your retirement funds with you when you separate service with them. This eliminates them from and mandatory distributions of funds and tax liabilities that may be incurred. They generally give you 60 days to transfer or take your money before it goes back into their retirement fund. During these 60 days, you may be advised to Roll Over your money into an IRA. A traditional IRA Account will have most of the same stipulations that the 400 series account had but it will allow your money to continue to grow if you do not have to use it at the time of retirement. Most IRA accounts are market-based investments as well and are subject to market risks. But they, like the 400 series are tax-deferred so you do not have to pay any tax on the funds until you begin distribution of the money. Also, depending on what type of account you choose to move your money to, you can continue to contribute to your IRA after it has been rolled over to help it to grow.

3. Withdraw all the $$$ - You can take a lump sum of your fund. This money will be considered income. This income is taxable and will be added to any other income you may earn at that time like Social Security or other income sources. Although there are a couple of caveats, if you withdraw before 59 ½ you are subject to tax penalties and interest deductions that will lessen the actual amount you can use for retirement expenses.

Leave it with your current employer and withdraw as desired - If your current employer allows the funds to stay with them, you have the option to leave the money there. However, remember the majority of 400 series accounts are market based (placed in the stock market to earn additional funds) and are subject to the risk of the market during the time the funds are there. If the market goes down, your retirement funds will go down possibly leaving you with less money to withdraw when needed. Also consider what may happen if your employer goes belly up, you potentially lose you money.

Here are some of the rules that apply to the 400 series. There are many different rules that may apply and may change annually. Here are a few that are consistent throughout.

1. 59 ½ is the minimum eligible age to begin taking withdrawals without a penalty. There is an exception. The Rule of 55. The Rule of 55 is a regulation set in place by the IRS that allows those 55 and older to withdraw funds from their 401(k) or 403(b) without receiving a tax penalty. The rule of 55 applies only if you have separated service from your employer.
    a. Let me give you a couple of examples Sam is currently working for XYZ company. He previously worked for ZYX company. Sam decides to leave ZYX at age 54. He leaves behind his 401k. ZYX does not allow Sam to roll over or transfer his money into another account. Sam is now 60 years old. He could have begun taking funds from his

ZYX account without any tax penalty at age 55 because he no longer works for them. Sam should consult a financial professional before beginning to withdraw these funds. Any money Sam takes from this account will be taxed at the current tax rate.

   b. Joe is 55 and works for ZYX. ZYX has changed hands. The new owners are allowing Joe to move his money to another account if he leaves their company. Joe also goes to work for XYZ company. Per the IRS rules, Joe can roll over this money into a like-kind account where the rules are the same as the rules that governed the funds previously. Joe still has the option to withdraw if he chooses but he can also keep the funds in a retirement plan until he is ready to retire. As you should, Joe decides to consult a financial professional before he begins to withdraw any funds to ensure he is reaching maximum benefit for his money.

2. Maximum contribution limits for 2021 is 19,500 and a bonus of up to $26000 at age 50.
3. You must have mandatory distribution of assets called RMD's (Required Mandatory Distribution's) at age 72 to avoid penalty. The IRS tax penalty for RMD's is 50% of the accumulated account. This is something you want to avoid.
4. Any withdrawals prior to 59 ½ must be approved by the employer following IRS Guidelines due to hardship and

will be subject to taxation. Early withdrawal for hardship may be allowed without penalty. The penalty for early withdrawal is 10%.

Last year in 2020 due to the COVID pandemic, the government allowed withdrawals of up to $100,000 from 400 series retirement plans, without penalty, to help offset the loss of wages, jobs, and business closures. That privilege has not currently been extended to any future years. However, consult with your financial professional to see what the status is for you.

CHAPTER 2

IRA'S VS ROTH IRA'S

People who do not have companies that provide them with one of The 400 series or Self-Employed Sub Contractors, or Small Business owners, may still want to establish a plan for their retirement. As stated in book 1, defined benefits or pensions are almost extinct. Social Security Income also seems to be on its last leg. "The 1980 replacement", The 400 series are great, but may not be the best option for today's financial climate. In the last 20+ years, financial strategies and plans have changed. Just like cars, there are new models and types to consider today. So, what are some of the chances of upgrades or different options that may be considered? One of which is a traditional IRA. These plans can be offered through market-based (when your money is invested in a mutual fund or the stock market) or safe money investments (when your money is invested mainly in insurance-based or indexed products). Both market-based and safe money accounts have similar IRS Regulations as the

400 series however the contributions limits are quite different. The contribution allotments may change annually so you must check every year. For the year 2021, the contribution limit is $6000 with a bonus of $1000 at age 50 and older. Because a traditional IRA is a tax-deferred account taxes will be paid on this account at the time of withdrawal of funds.

Additionally, some options allow for "Tax-Free" Contributions. What does that mean? It means that you pay the taxes for this fund upfront or in the year that you are contributing so that when you withdraw funds at retirement there is no tax obligation. The type of account that allows this is called a ROTH IRA.

Here are some additional benefits to having a ROTH IRA:

There are no required minimum distributions for Roth IRAs during your lifetime. That means when you turn 70 ½ or older the IRS does not require you to take money out of your account. In a traditional IRA like the 400 series if you do not start taking money out at that age you may incur a tax penalty of 50%. Uncle Sam will get his money one way or the other. That also means you can let the money keep growing until you need it, or even leave tax-free income to your beneficiaries. This is a great thing!

The Roth is especially beneficial for younger people who typically have lower income tax rates than they are likely to have when they withdraw Roth IRA funds. In layman's terms, that means they will pay less tax now than when they retire. They also have decades for their money to compound before retirement, allowing them to take greater advantage of compound interest. This means like any savings plan, the longer you save the more money you will earn on your savings. And there are no age limits for creating a Roth IRA, so one can be created for a child of any age. Just like the new Mercedes, the updates are looking good. But just like anything that goes up there are some downsides.

Downsides to the ROTH

- For the tax year 2020: An individual's ability to contribute to a Roth IRA starts phasing out at $124,000 and disappears altogether at $139,000. For couples, the contribution is reduced at $196,000 and phased out altogether at $206,000.
- For tax year 2021: The phase-out range for an individual is $125,000 to $140,000. For couples, it is $198,000 to $208,000.
- This amount changes every year, so you need to check with your Tax representative to see what the Income amounts are for the current year.

Finally, to qualify for a ROTH the funds must come from a source that indicates the funds have already been taxed like a bank account or savings plan. If you are more of a spender than a saver this may be a problem for you. Like the traditional IRA, there are various types of accounts to choose from. A financial professional can help you to choose the best plan for you.

So, what happens if you have a Traditional IRA, and you want a ROTH IRA?

I thought you would never ask. If your income limits allow you can have both. If not, you can do what is called a **ROTH Conversion**. This means you can change or convert your traditional IRA to a ROTH. When that is done you pay the tax on the amount that you are converting at the time it is withdrawn. Let me give you an example.

You have $100,000 in a Traditional IRA. You are 59 ½ years old and you want to retire at 65. Your financial advisor has advised you based on the current trends that taxes will be higher at age 65. Your children are past dependent age and you do not have any other right offs for your income taxes that can be considered to lower your income at retirement. If social security stays in tack your income at age 65 will be the same as you are receiving now. Your professional says you should consider options that will lessen how much tax you pay at retirement. So, for the next five years, it is suggested that you take $20,000 from your IRA and put it into a ROTH Conversion – an account where you pay taxes now. Paying the tax now will avoid you having to pay tax on that income at retirement. That is an exciting consideration. Just remember taking $20,000 today will increase your income today and increase your tax obligation, but hopefully what you pay now will be less than what you would have to pay in the future. That is what financial professionals prepare you to bank on and should be able to show you the contrast. Remember consulting with an expert will help you make the right decisions.

Now as an extension of the IRA saga, **Ladies you need to be aware!**

More than 11.6 million firms and businesses are owned by women, employing nearly 9 million people, and generating $1.7 trillion in sales as of 2017. The growing number of women needing retirement coverage is especially important to pay attention to. Once again, the 400 series have been the "go-to" when considering retirement planning for Women in Business and Women Business Owners. Although the same rules apply, some extremely specific things apply to women that need to be considered when planning for retirement.

Here is a list of the top statistics to consider:

- Everywhere in the world women live longer than men. This means women will need retirement income for more years than men.
- Women generally make less money than men - Jul 29, 2019, PayScale reports.
- It is commonly said that half of all marriages end in divorce. Although, in most cases, women may receive some type of spousal support from the divorce, spousal support in divorce is more often being paid by women than ever before.
- Health care will cost more for women than men during retirement.
- COVID-19 has set women way back. The risk of mothers leaving the labor force and reducing work hours to assume caretaking responsibilities amounts to $64.5 billion per year in lost wages and economic activity. Four times as many women as men dropped out of the labor

force in September 2020, roughly 865,000 women compared with 216,000 men. Women affected in the short term will also feel the long-term effects on their retirement security.

- Women have fewer alternative sources of income after retirement than men, and they are more likely to rely on Social Security retirement and disability benefits. Because Social Security benefits are based on lifetime earnings and the Social Security Administration calculates the average indexed monthly earnings during the 35 years in which the worker earned the most, if a woman takes time out of the workforce or reduces work hours and receives lower pay, it affects her retirement benefits. In addition, if she has fewer than 35 years of earnings, then the years of zero earnings are included among the 35 averaged years, lowering the lifetime average. Decisions to leave the workforce or reduce hours—or the impact of becoming unemployed because of a recession—will not only affect Social Security but also the likelihood of women holding pensions or other employer-based retirement plans.
- Adults ages 45 to 64 are the most likely to be caregivers. About a quarter (23%) of adults ages 45 to 64 cares for an aging adult. A significant share of adults ages 65 and older – 17% – serve as caregivers for another aging American. These adults, who themselves are advanced in age, are the second most likely age group to be caregivers. Many in this group are caring for a spouse or partner (29%) or a friend or neighbor (33%)

What does this mean for women?

With all the additional challenges women face as business owners and employees, the sooner you begin to prepare for your retirement, the better it is for you. So "They say", you will live longer, you will make less money, and you may have to take care of more people than yourself on a predominately smaller income even though you are in your retirement years. Not a pretty picture at all. But you can change it, you do not have to be one of the many women who fall in the category of "unprepared." Forewarned is forearmed.

Here is the silver lining. The bright side is, the sooner you begin to prepare, you can change the picture, making things a little clearer and making it better for yourself can happen. Your contributions will be manageable, and you will have a longer time to contribute towards your goals. More than anything these statics identify the need for women to have supplemental income sources to help with lifestyle maintenance at retirement. If you have not begun to consider retirement as a real thing that you need to plan for and pay attention to…. This is your wake-up call!

CHAPTER 3

CASH VALUE LIFE INSURANCE

The best keep secret that gets the worse wrap ever. Does anyone remember when middle age to elderly males came to your door, rang the doorbell, came in, set down on the couch with the plastic on it, and collected your $8.50 for the insurance policy? After his cup of coffee and a brief chat, he wrote your receipt nodded his hat, and left until next month. Cost may be different, but most people can remember this "kneecap to kneecap" picture of their life insurance agent. Okay, fast forward out of the '50s and '60s for most. After many battles, in 1979 a new mindset came into the insurance industry. The statement "Buy Term and Invest the Difference" was the mantra of the era. During that time whole life insurance was what most were buying. The constraints and the policies at that time, although they were perceived the best for that season, were not as good as they should have been. Whole life insurance, the initial cash value life insurance, required you to pay on the account for as long as you had the policy, to keep it "in force "(active). At some point, you would have paid more into the policy than the amount needed to pay for the insurance. Any amounts paid over the cost of insurance and administrative fees were considered cash value and could be paid to you in dividends or could be borrowed from the policy to use as needed for a nominal fee. Enter A.L Williams and the reinvention of what we now call Temporary or "Term" insurance. William's goal was to get people to see that there was a better way to secure life insurance protection. The assumption being the only purpose of life insurance was to protect your loved ones, by replaces the loss of income upon death. At the time Williams began his campaign other options would generate more income for the client than adding cash to an insurance policy. The stock market was soaring, and mutual funds were all the crazes. 401k's have begun to catch on and were accepted by the IRS as a viable retirement supplemental alternative. The mindset was buying insurance for only the time you may need it for a lesser cost and use the remaining dollars that would have been put into the life insurance cash value to into a higher earning investment. The idea was great, and millions bought and are still buying into it. As long as the market was/is booming this can be a great way to make money for retirement. Many prominent financial advisors still support the fact saying the Insurance should be for protection only. After your kids are grown and out of the house and can provide for themselves, there is no need for large amounts of insurance for your whole life. Additionally, investments should be a separate financial plan. The ideology of A. L. Williams was the catalyst for many other major insurance firms. The largest of which still promotes his core ideas is Primerica.

The best keep secret that gets the worse wrap ever. Does anyone remember when middle age to elderly male came to your door, rang the doorbell, came in, set down on the couch with the plastic on it and collected your $8:50 cents for the insurance policy? After his cup of coffee and a brief chat he wrote your receipt nodded his hat and left until next month. Cost may be different, but most people can remember this "kneecap to kneecap" picture of their life insurance agent. Ok fast forward out of the 50's and 60's for most. After many battles, in 1979 a new mindset came into the insurance industry. The statement "Buy Term and Invest the Difference" was the mantra of the era. During that time whole life insurance was what most were buying. The constraints and the policies at that time, although they were perceived the best for that season, were not as good as they should have been. Whole life insurance, the initial cash value life insurance, required you to pay on the account for as long as you had the policy, to keep it "in force "(active). At some point you would have paid more into the policy than the amount needed to pay for the insurance. Any amounts paid over the cost of insurance and administrative fees was considered cash value and could be paid to you in dividends or could be borrowed from the policy to use as needed for a nominal fee. Enter A.L

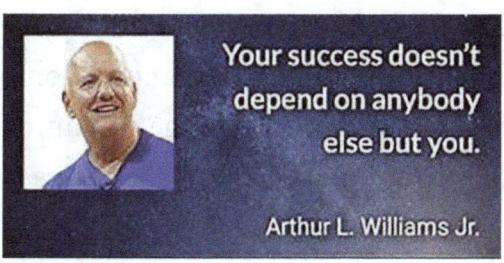

Williams and the reinvention of what we now call Temporary or "Term" insurance. William's goal was to get people to see that there was a better way to secure life insurance protection. The assumption being the only purpose of life insurance was to protect your loved ones, by replaces loss of income upon death. At the time Williams began his campaign there were other options that would generate more income for the client than adding cash to an insurance policy. The stock market was soaring, and mutual funds were all the crazes. 401k's have begun to catch on and was accepted by the IRS as a viable retirement supplemental alternative. The mindset was buying insurance for only the time you may need it for a lessor cost and use the remaining dollars that would have been put into the life insurance cash value to into a higher earning investment. The idea was great, and millions bought and are still buying into it. As long as the market was/is booming this can be a great way to make money for retirement. Many prominent financial advisors still support the fact saying the Insurance should be for protection only. After your kids are grown and out of the house and can provide for themselves, there is no need for large amounts of insurance for your whole life. Additionally, investments should be separate financial plan. The ideology of A. L. Williams was the catalyst for many other major insurance firms. The largest of which who still promotes his core ideas is Primerica.

Phase 2: Along comes 2001, 2008, and most recently 2017-2018. The stock market crashes. The downturn in the market causes the country to go into recession/depression. Millions of people lost millions of dollars from their investments. Buy term invest the difference took a major hit. How does this affect retirement specifically your retirement? Most 400 series accounts are invested in the stock market so if the market tanks, so do these types of retirement account. Also remember as we have discussed previously many financial advisors state even if the market suffers a loss, you should have the time to make your money back if you just wait it out. The biggest challenge with that mindset is, you never know when the market will dip, nor how long it will stay down, nor how old you will be when it happens, or where you will be in your retirement phase when it does. The truth is you may or may not have time to recover any losses. Most retirees do not want to take that chance.

So, what are the alternatives to these types of risk? Many financial advisors suggest that one major alternative is the newly updated indexed cash value life insurance. Their primary offset to market risk is that your life insurance policy's cash value is not in the stock market, so you do not have the risk of loss. Plus, because the earning potential is based on stock market indexes you earn a much higher rate of return than you would by simply investing in a regular savings account or a certificate of deposit. These types of investments are called safe money investments because the potential for loss is very minimal. Most new cash value life insurance policies also offer additional benefits call accelerated benefits that include options for tax-free withdrawals which means any money taken from the policy cannot be taxed because all the taxes have already been paid, that can be used for caregiving expenses if the client cannot perform 2 of the 6 daily living activities such as bathing or feeding yourself.

Some benefits may help with long-term care facility expenses. There are also benefits that may help with critical illness and injury. Additionally, your cash value is accessible to you to use for whatever you choose.

Let me give you a few real-life examples. In another life, I was the co-owner/founder of an independent Gospel record label. During that season promotion and distribution, deals were what most independents sought. To get the label off the ground we needed capital. Unlike many, we were destined not to use drug dollars to fuel our start-up. So, we turned to angel investors. One of the investors a very savvy hipster from Newport Beach used dollars from an indexed universal life insurance policy to sure up our efforts. Our little start-up business was bought out by a major label and went on to make history in the Gospel Music community. The moral to the story is a tax-free investment from a cash value life insurance policy helped to propel my career.

One of my colleagues was injured on the job before the normal retirement age. Forced to take early retirement due to disability their pension allotment was much less than expected. The injured person had taken out an indexed universal life insurance policy that had cans value accumulation. The cash value in the policy is currently being used to help supplement the loss of income due to the injury. The family can maintain their lifestyle because of the cash value that can use from the policy. The best thing about it is that that income from the policy will come to them tax-free until they are 120 years old or until they pass away.

Finally, one of my clients recently got married. Originally, they set up a cash value life insurance policy to help supplement their retirement. They used a portion of their cash value to help pay for their wedding Their policy is still in place. They are still contributing to it. But they are not able to use the dollars as a retirement supplemental but for current-day necessities. Like I said a best-kept secret.

Many naysayers will say the fees and the cost of insurance for these types of policies are much higher than necessary. However, they do not explain the fees for the cost of investing in mutual funds or the stock market. Nor do they explain that after vesting (normally 10-12 years) most administrative fees for cash value life insurance policies go away or are greatly reduced.

They also do not explain that the cost of insurance is the same for every type of policy. It does not matter whether it is a permanent (whole life or indexed) or temporary (term) policy. Salespeople sell that is their job. But each type of life insurance has its place. The goal for you as a reader is to find a financial advisor that you can trust that will educate you on all areas (400 series, Insurance plans, investments, and Individual Retirement Plans) that may/will provide you the best benefit for your retirement. And Ladies remember, cash value life insurance is impartial. It works, the same for men as it does for women. A diverse portfolio (a combination of investment strategies and supplementals) is always a good way to go when planning for retirement.

Somethings to pay close attention to when looking to the 400 series and or Life Insurance:

When considering the 400 series ask if your employer will match any of your contributions. Also, ask how long you must work for your company to qualify for the plan. Some employers have a period before you invest in their retirement plan. Once the vesting period is met; any employee can enter the plan. Generally, there are no medical requirements to meet when joining these plans. Like group life insurance, these may be benefits offered by the company as incentives to gain and retain good employees.

When considering life insurance, the first thing to know is you may need to take a medical exam. Insurance underwriting and approval guidelines are not automatic like the 400 series. You must be approved to secure any type of policy whether it be Term or Perm. Additionally, your driving record and financial background may be considered when approving policies. Some people may not qualify but most do. Secondly, age is a factor when calculating the cost of Insurance. Morbidity - analysis of medical condition and Mortality- how long you may live, play into the calculation. In plain English, the older you are the more the insurance will cost.

Bottom line: consider age, health, and lifestyle when seeking insurance as a supplemental for retirement and protection.

Segment 3 will discuss more specific advantages you may have when planning for retirement if you have a defined benefit or pension. We will also talk about some health care and social security nuisances. Our hope is this trilogy will be a pocket resource that can be utilized when considering options for retirement.

Final Words

Key Take-aways:

- ⇨ Men have different needs at retirement than women.
- ⇨ Women live longer than men.
- ⇨ ROTH options are a good strategy for tax efficiency at retirement.
- ⇨ Cash-value life insurance is also an option that should be considered for tax efficiency during retirement.
- ⇨ Start planning as early as you can.
- ⇨ This is a mini resource. For more in-depth information check out the podcast "I'm your Agent" at https://podcasts.apple.com/us/podcast/imyouragentpodcast/id1531948189 and seek a financial professional to assist with setting up a retirement or retirement supplemental plan.

**BOOK 1
SEGMENT 3**

THE RETIREMENT TRILOGY:

A BOOK SERIES WITH WRITTEN ADAPTATIONS FROM THE "I'M YOUR AGENT PODCAST"

A podcast geared towards education, information and allowing you to retire on your own terms

---

INTRODUCTION

You made it to segment three. Congratulations! Now let me provide you with some nuances that will help you move to a better place for your financial future. As promised this book will talk about specific advantages geared towards specific groups of people that will help increase your current and future investments. I will also give some insight on what retirees do not see as major priorities in retirement. Book three talks more about specific advantages you may have when planning for retirement if you have a pension. I will also talk about some health care and social security nuisances. Additionally, I will talk about a specific strategy for people who want to contribute higher contributions than allowed in traditional retirement vehicles. I will complete this part of the effort by sharing about legacy building and different ways to "pay it forward" for loved ones and others. My hope is this is a resource that can be utilized when considering options for future retirement goals.

SEGMENT 3
TABLE OF CONTENT

Chapter 1   Cover Me: What you should look to cover in Retirement.

Chapter 2   Pension Maximization

Chapter 3   Kai-Zen

Chapter 4   Retiring from the Military

Chapter 5   It is about more than money – Legacy Building.

CHAPTER 1

COVER ME: WHAT YOU SHOULD LOOK TO COVER IN RETIREMENT.

Ladies and gentlemen, this information is not new. Most of you have heard these words, seen these concepts, and even practiced some of these methods. But it is always good to review, revisit and update information. Just like with preventive medicine, it is always a good practice to get a checkup. It helps to discover any pending ailments and/or keeps a well-maintained body in shape. Just like vehicle servicing keeps your car in good running condition for as long as possible, without an oil change or regular maintenance, you may have more costly repairs or even worse find yourself sitting on the side of the road waiting for a tow to help you out.

Something else to consider, when visiting the dealership for maintenance while you wait you may find yourself visiting the showroom. This allows you to see what new models may be available. Look at this chapter as your service manual and your visit to the showroom. It will provide you with a brief overview of what you and your advisor should look for when developing your initial retirement supplemental strategy.

Here is what your plan should cover:

- Income plan - where your day-to-day income will come from
- Investment plan - strategies on how to grow wealth and income during this period.
- Taxes – what will your tax obligations be, what income do you have that will be taxed, and at what rate. Offsetting tax liability with Tax-deferred and after-tax ("Tax-Free") income.
- Lifestyle plan – what activity will you have once retired? Will you continue to work?
- Heath Care plan – Will you have to pay for any health care expenses? How much and how long? Will your

employer continue to pay for all or part of your health care coverage?
- General Long Term Care Plan – Will your Health care plan cover Long Term Care Cost? Do you have any supplemental Long Term Care Coverage?
- Legacy Plan – Do you plan to leave a legacy for your family? If so who and how much? Will you have legacy contributions for Charity?

Your personal plan may include all or part of these items. Experts greatly recommend including each phase of this outline in your plan to insure comprehensive and complete coverage. It is also greatly recommended that you do not try completing this plan without expert assistance. That may mean a team of advisors. But more than anything it means to seek creditable help at the beginning, during, and at the end of the process.

Here are some key things every retiree will face.

*When it comes to expenses, you will incur your biggest expenses in these areas during these ages.

- 50 to 65 your biggest expense will be housing - Where to live at retirement, downsize, take on boarders, live with children, can you still facilitate your mortgage – your biggest expense when considering retirement.
- 66 to 75 your biggest expense will be medical cost - Medicare/Medicaid supplements are subject to government approval and expenditure. Currently, they only cover up to 80% of medical costs for seniors. A minimum

of 20% will need to be covered by the retiree. One other thing to note is most prescription drugs are not covered by these plans if you make over what is considered "low income" so the cost of your prescription may be in addition to the 20% outlay.

- 76 and older Long-Term Care (LTC) may be your biggest concern - After the first 10 years medical expenses and LTC takes on your biggest worry. People are living longer. 1 out of every 5 seniors will need some type of LTC during retirement. Most often these costs last 3-5 years. In 2020 average costs were upwards of $8,000 per month. Most medical insurance has limited to no coverage for LTC costs.

*Ages and times may vary per individual. When it comes to expenses, you will incur your biggest expenses in these areas during these ages.

75% of people in today's market still do not have retirement plans – income, lifestyle, or legacy – most have not considered these expenses, nor have they planned for them. How to save and when to begin will always be an ongoing plight.

If you are expecting your employer's medical coverage to support that 20% here is something to consider there may be a co-payment for these plans and the plan coverage may still not meet the full 20% needed to cover the full cost. This will greatly depend on the plan coverage your employer offers and the election you choose when picking a change.

CHAPTER 2

PENSION MAXIMIZATION

Let's begin this chapter with three simple things.

1. How many people have pensions?
2. What is Pension Maximization?
3. Who can get it?

Because this is a specific opportunity geared towards a select group, it is especially important to define who that group is and what that means to the general population. The percentage of workers covered by a traditional pension – paying a lifetime income through an annuity is generally based on an employee's years of service and final income or wage calculation. In the last 25 years, the number of these types of plans has declined from 38% to 20%. Additionally, only 4% of private-sector workers have this type of benefit plan as their only plan down from 60% in the 1980s.

The question now becomes, if you are in the unique group of having a pension, wouldn't you want to get the most benefit that you could? If that is the case, then you need to understand this group narrows even further.

Pension Maximation is only for Married People.

Investoco.com defines Pension maximization as a retirement strategy for couples whereby they choose the highest possible annuity payout for one spouse's lifetime while obtaining life insurance to provide income for the surviving spouse. Pension maximization requires a life-only annuity and life insurance.

A spouse is a significant other in a marriage, civil union, or common-law marriage. The term is gender-neutral, whereas a male spouse is a husband, and a female spouse is a wife. As of 2020, Domestic Partners are not considered "family" by law, although there are some workplaces and companies that will qualify domestic partners for these same rights. Even if a domestic partnership is not recognized in your state, your employer may allow your partner to receive employer benefits. When considering pension maximization please check with your employer to confirm if your partner qualifies for this provision.

Pension Maximization requires a blend of employer benefit payout and cash value life insurance. The strategy must have both components. It also must have enough time to build appropriate cash to make the plan work efficiently. Although you can begin the process at any time, if you choose this strategy, the sooner you begin the better.

Here is an example of how the strategy may be used most effectively in California. A teacher in the Los Angeles Unified School District (LAUSD), one of the companies that still offer a defined benefit plan, will receive $6,500 per month from his pension before tax. Using the benefits calculator from CALSTRS (the State-funded pension system for teachers in California) he finds out to leave his spouse 100% of his pension he would have to deduct $1000 per month from his pension distribution to supplement the administration of this process. This would bring the amount that goes to both of you at retirement and your spouse upon your demise to $5500 per month for life.

In its simplest form what Pension Maximization does is take that same $1000 you would offset to CALSTRS and invests it in a cash value life insurance product normally for 10 to 15 years (instead of a lifetime). Your original distribution benefit increases back to $6500 after the 10-15 year buy-in. You and your spouse will have the benefit of using the accumulated cash value in the life insurance policy if necessary. If not, your spouse will receive the lump sum of the death benefit to utilize. Additionally, there are benefit riders that will help cover LTC and medical costs if needed. It can be a great benefit for the right couple; however, it is not a fit for everyone. When considering Pension Maximization, a financial advisor is highly recommended.

CHAPTER 3

KAI - ZEN

The chapter is an incredibly special strategy for people with a consistent income of 6 figures or more (average income requirement begins at $150k per year). Athletes, Entertainers, Small Business Owners, Health Care Professionals, Legal Professionals, and others with sizeable sums to invest for 15 years have benefited greatly from this opportunity.

I first investigated this strategy when a friend of mine who is a sports agent and attorney shared the idea with me and wanted my input. After that, my company began to offer the opportunity and provided more information. I did my due diligence, and this was the first thing I found.

Kai-Zen is a Long-Term Investment and commitment.

If you are looking for instant gratification Kai-Zen is not vehicle. This option works best for long term planning goals. Some companies even utilize this strategy for its key employee's and executives as a bonus, or as part of their retirement plan strategy. Let's begin by defining what Kai-Zen is, and then move into how it works.

The word *"KAIZEN" means improvement.* Moreover, it means continuing improvement in personal life, home life, social life, and working life. When applied to the workplace KAIZEN means continuing improvement involving everyone – managers and workers alike." (Kaizen Institute, Ltd.)

The purpose of this segment is for you to "Kaizen" spiritually, mentally, physically and most of all with your retirement planning strategy.

As it relates to retirement, Kai-Zen is a strategy that helps one maintain their current lifestyle in the event of a chronic illness, premature death, or an inability to sufficiently save for retirement. Due to limitations, traditional retirement plans are typically insufficient for high-income earners. The Kai-Zen strategy helps to eliminate this insufficiency without putting a drain on one's current finances.

Kai-Zen is the ONLY strategy that uses leverage to help you acquire more of the benefits you need to financially protect yourself and your family. Its unique fusion of financing and life insurance offers you more protection and the potential to earn more for retirement than you could obtain without leverage. Leverage in this case means funding/financing provided by banking institutions.

The Kai-Zen Strategy is simple. Premiums are jointly funded by bank financing and the participant or employer (participant). This is a 15-year Investment. The participant contributes for 5-years, the bank matches your initial 5-years contribution, and then makes all contributions for the next 5-years. Your investment is in a life insurance policy. This policy secures the bank's funding. In 15 years, you receive 100% of what has been earned in the account minus any bank contributions. Your principal investment triples during that time.

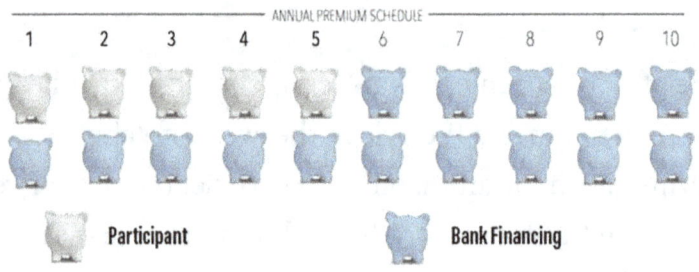

Here are three examples of how Kai-Zen may be used most effectively: As we previously discussed in a traditional 400 series such as 401k, 403b, or 457. the maximum retirement contribution is $19,500 for 2021. You choose to max out your contribution every year however you are still overly concerned as to whether you will have enough money to fully support your retirement. Your annual income is $150k per year or more. You receive an inheritance from your grandmother of $500k. You plan to retire in 15 years and want a great investment for your newfound wealth. After careful consideration and communication with your financial advisor, you choose to invest the funds in a Kai-Zen Plan. For 5 years, you invest $100k each year into the account. The bank matches your contribution. For the next five years, the bank continues to contribute to your account. In 10 years, your initial $500k investment has now become $1.5m leaving you with peace of mind when you retire.

Example two: You are a new professional athlete with a 3-year contract on a major sports team. You are healthy and have had some great but limited playing time. You have high hopes of renegotiation of your contract, within the next two years. Your initial 5-year contract provided you 600k per year after taxes and expenses. Over the last three years, you have secured three moderate endorsement deals which have yielded you after taxes and expenses $3M per endorsement. Currently, you have chosen to live off your funds without any major investments that could have yielded a sizable return. Outside of a small stock and bitcoin investment portfolio, you have purchased two properties, you bought a car and some other toys. Nothing extravagant but all the things you would expect a young athlete would do when coming into this kind of success. You still have some funds to live on and a comfortable lump sum in the bank. This year you have a $7M endorsement secured and you have chosen to be more aggressive about your investments. After consulting with your management team, you have decided to contribute 500k per year for five years from the most recent campaign. With the bank's matches in 15 years, you would be guaranteed a $7.5M investment in a tax-deferred/after-tax vehicle which provided, cash value, a death benefit, and supplemental medical benefits for the rest of your life.

Example three: You are a Chief Executive Officer for a small but successful law firm. As a part of your Retirement package, your company contract includes a Kai-Zen plan. After you are vested (5 years of service to the company) you will receive $250k per year in a Kai-Zen account. If separation of service should come before the 5-year contribution is completed, you will have the option to continue the contributions on your own. The company's contribution would be $1.25m making your retirement investment $3.75m at retirement age.

All these examples show very conservative but realistic outcomes. An important thing to note here is the ability to contribute large amounts with the same IRS code security as any other cash value insurance policy. Also, important to note is if the client qualifies for this type of account there will be accelerated benefit riders attached that could assist with medical costs and LTC coverage if needed. Furthermore, there is cash value availability from this account in 15 years. This can be far shorter than other investments. Unlike traditional retirement plan designs, you are protected from loss. Because it is purchased with after-tax dollars, there are no tax ramifications. Kai-Zen is a non-recourse loan from the financial institution meaning that there is no penalty attached to the financing. Upon approval, the only condition is that you make your contribution for 5 years.

Because of the vesting period of 15 years Kai-Zen generally works best for those ages 30-55 but there is no actual age limit to invest in the plan. And it is an exceptionally good way to build a legacy for your family and others.

This strategy if implement should be considered an asset to building wealth like any other income growth strategy. And, because it is an insurance policy protected against loss with guaranteed tax advantages under IRS Code 7702, you can have as many of these types of plans that your income and suitability will support.

CHAPTER 4

THE MILITARY

Between 2021 and 2031, 2.28 million people will retire from the United States Military

To all veterans, thank you for your service and for protecting our country. For career military, you have a unique quandary. Most people enter the military between the ages of 17 and 24. After 20 years of service, you are eligible to retire. That would make you between the ages of 37 to 44. You are still incredibly young when it comes to the traditional retirement age. The military does offer a pension. Most military retirees are 20 to 25 years younger than the standardized retiree. The good thing is that the military pension is unlike most pensions because it allows you to withdraw funds as soon as you retire. Your pension is based on your highest rank in military service upon departing service.

Your health care benefits are paid until age 65 through Tricare and after 65 through Tricare for life. Part or all these benefits are paid for by the retiree at a discounted cost. The quality and quantity of these benefits must be reviewed and discussed with your branch of service. Additional benefits may include home buying assistance packages and college funds for you or your children.

Just like other pensions, the one thing that is true about your military pension and benefit plan is that it may only cover up to 70% of your active military salary. The fact that you have so many more years to live you may need additional income to maintain your lifestyle. Most retired military personnel seek additional employment. That puts them right back in the pool of other retirees. This gives them the necessity to generate additional funds to sustain their lifestyle, and the need to find other outlets (work, school, business ownership, etc.) to fulfill their life's purpose and legacy. Planning for retirement should be a big part of any military member's future. It should be a necessity, not an option. Seeking assistance and advisement for your retirement planning should also be a top priority when considering retiring.

CHAPTER 5

IT IS ABOUT MORE THAN MONEY – LEGACY BUILDING.

Here are some simple reminders as to what pre retirees and retirees face.

- Only 5% of celebrities (actors, musicians, athletes, artists) make a living with their chosen profession. Most get

or have regular employment while trying to live their dream.
- Less than 2% of seniors use reverse mortgages or home equity as an additional retirement income source. This is greatly due to refinancing, causing loss of equity in the property so they do not qualify.
- 38% of seniors move to other states at retirement. This may help with lowering expenses at retirement.
- Although some may consider this option, 68% of retirees choose not to downsize – move to a smaller home - at retirement.

In segments 1 and 2, we discussed more the who and the what of a retirement strategy. Simon Sinex, largely known for his presentations on TED Talks said, "People don't buy what you do, they buy why you do it". I tend to agree with him. In this chapter of book 3, the discussion will be more about the why of the retirement strategy. Specifically, reasons why these tips and the need for an activity plan are so important. When you look at the chapters geared towards Women, Entertainers/Athletes, Small Business and Clergy it is easy to see the "why" - to secure a lifestyle after their career (generally 80 to 90 percent of their highest 3-year income).

But there must be something else after income is earned. Life must be more than just about making money.

This "something else" must take as much dedication and consideration as your financial strategy choices. It will take a clear-cut reason as to "why" it should happen. The "why" for retirement planning is not in the future. Although it prepares for future events, IT IS NOW! I think Beyonce' said it best when she said, "I was here". I would not only say I was here, but I "hear". Did you leave a mark and did people hear what that mark was saying? Did they hear something you said or did what you said make a difference in their lives?

That is why it is a great idea to write your plans down and make them plain. A great book I read says it like this "Then the Lord said: write the vision and make it plain on tablets so that a herald may run with it" Habakkuh2:2. This is not a bible study, but a 2021 translation adaptation does apply. The Lord being the ruler or person in charge, (in this illustration that is you) makes a decree or a decision, to write down how he/she sees things happening in the future so the people after them can read it, run with it, and fulfill any aspects that may not have been completed at the time of origin and during the remainder of their life.

Additionally, what is interesting about this verse, is that The Lord or the person of origin tells someone else to document "in writing" the activity. That means a tangible document that can be passed along. It does not say he or she has help with what his or her vision is. But he or she does have help putting what they think should happen in an orderly, structured written form. This will allow others to bring the vision to life and continue the vision through their lives. That scribe or person documenting the vision sounds like an advisor or a team of advisors. The document also sounds like a will, living trust, health care directive, financial income plan, lifestyle plan, and/or Legacy plan.

"The Herald" in this case is the person or persons that is/are translating this message/ written document verbally to others (family, friends, loved one's charities, etc.). This person should also be a trusted advisor. The product that is produced from the vision is the actual plan that is reviewed revised, re-read, re-written, and ran with. That is the essence of "Pay it Forward" or Legacy.

"Always pay it forward, and never forget to pay it back. It's how you got here, and it defines where you're going…" Brian Solis

---

Legacy means something transmitted by or received from an ancestor or predecessor from the past. Legacy uses the past to determine the future. Legacy answers the question of What is in it for me. That way at the end of the day, no one has any question as to what they may or may not receive in this life as well as their life after yours. Your descendants are receiving, learning, and growing through things passed on from predecessors.

From a common-sense perspective, it only makes sense that after 30 years (give or take) of generating an income through some form of employment, entrepreneurship, or sports/entertainment activity you are now transitioning into a 3rd or 4th stage of life. What will you do? Let's bring it closer to home, after 30 years of a to-do list, and people telling you what to and how to do things, how will you do that now that those sources aren't there? After walking into the office with the coffee made and an assistant asking you if you want a cup, who will do that for you now? After 30 years in and out of hotels, on buses, planes, trains, and cars; After seeing so many cities in a week that you do not know which one you are in; After eating in restaurants, hotel lobbies, and room service when you finally say I am going home to sleep in my bed, eat my food, who will cook and clean for you? Emphasis on "YOU have to do that". And the bigger realization is if it has not been you, but it will be you now, is that may take some getting used to. After waking up every day at 4:30 am for a mandatory workout/training session, you finally get to choose whether you will keep that schedule or not, what will you do? You finally have the choice to do you without reservation, what will that look like?

Ladies and gentlemen, these things are just as much a part of your retirement plan and legacy as "will you have enough money to live on". Let me give you some stats that make these kinds of questions even more pertinent.

- 6 in 10 people over 50 provide financial support and care to other family members.
- Many studies show that 40% of people retire earlier than they plan with the #1 reason being health issues for themselves or a loved one. And the #1 cause is Alzheimer's.

This happened to my family on two different occasions in two different ways. The first time it occurred was when my father had a stroke due to high blood pressure. My father, a general contractor, had been self-employed most of my life. He did well or so I thought. My mother had always worked as well. For all my life, she worked for the County of Los Angeles. Her great county job afforded my family health care coverage. My parents were old school. A child was to stay in their place. My brother and I were not a part of the financial planning for the home. So, after 62 years of his life, my dad had a stroke. It was at that time that my mother decided to retire early to take care of him. My mother's HR representative showed her income would only change by $300 a month if she retired early, so she did.

The second time, my youngest brother after 25 years of service with the County of Los Angeles found himself with an unexpected debilitating illness. My brother seldom went to the doctor and thought he never needed any medical attention. He believed any illness could be fixed with vitamin c, aspirin, or alcohol (rubbing and drinking).

At age 56 the illness took its toll. He became bedridden. For as long as he could he worked from home but at some point, his debilitation caused him to have to retire. He had planned to retire at age 65, causing a shortfall in his planned pension funds by 8-9 years. He passed shortly after his 60th birthday.

My brother was very stubborn about adapting change especially when it would cost him money. I did my best to share with him the necessity of supplemental retirement planning and different options for income/medical care sources. He rejected my communication saying he was okay. He had all he needed. The county would take good care of him. As his illness worsened, he like many others then wanted to know about options but with a preexisting condition, he did not qualify. He became the statistic. He lived 3 ½ years bedridden needing LTC assistance. He had to absorb most of the cost. His resistance and procrastination put an unnecessary strain on his finances. Even with his great county insurance plan which thankfully took care of hospitalization, he still had to pay out of pocket for in-home care and other medical expenses.

The question then becomes who will be that person that retires early to take care of your loved one? For my family, it was my mother. If it is you, will you be healthy enough to do so? Also, will you have outlets to help you relieve the newly acquired stress that comes with the care that may be necessary? What is your health (mental and physical) plan to support and maintain your lifestyle once you retire? Why should you prepare this way? It is a part of your legacy. It not only helps others literally, but it also shows or teaches others how to help others in the future. It "Pays it forward".

Here are some other questions to ask yourself.

- Will you go back to school?
- Will you take on a second career?
- Will you increase your community service?
- Will you take on consulting, virtual training or open a business?

- Will you vacation for two months, buy a new car, downsize your home, or buy a new home?
- Or will you sit at home and binge watch television?

Whatever it is, write it down and make it plain. That way your efforts can continue to grow when you move on.

Interesting enough in today's world the documents most used to outline legacy or for writing the vision are called Wills, or Trusts (could be Living Wills or Living Trusts)

These vehicles provide directives on what you want to be done while alive, in case of incompetence or upon death. The challenging part is that most people do not take the time to put the information in writing. Some cultures are afraid to document directives or distribution of assets. Some people do not want to make plans for not living as though death or transition is not a part of life. Some people just do not feel the need as they do not plan to leave anything to others.

Here are some stats about Wills and Trusts:

- Only 4 out of 10 people have a will or a trust.
- 80% of people who have trust have not funded the trust (the will or the trust does not say who gets what when and why financially)

Final Words

- *If you fail to plan, you are planning to fail.*
  Benjamin Franklin

- *Plan your execution. Execute your plan.*
  Anonymous

Nothing happens if you do not run with the words. You must execute to have an impact. I received this text today. Do not confuse information with transformation. Transformation requires action. It does not matter what you know, it is what you do with that knowledge that makes you Great!

In the words of "Spock" from Star Trek (the tv series) "Live Long and Prosper". Then share that prosperity with those you love and those who need it! I hope you have gleaned from this trilogy. If you have any questions, need more information, or need help with planning, please contact me. Jefflyn Dangerfield, imyouragentpc@gmail.com. If I cannot help you, I am sure I know someone who can.

- This book is a resource. For more in-depth information check out the podcast "I'm your Agent" at **https://podcasts.apple.com/us/podcast/imyouragentpodcast/id1531948189** and *seek a financial professional to assist* with setting up retirement or retirement supplemental plan.

ABOUT THE AUTHOR

As a Retirement Specialist with Encore FFS, Jefflyn's passion is serving **Educators, Firefighters, Police Officers, Faith-Based Organizations, and Small Business Owners**. Her foremost focus is to provide her clients with optimal outcomes and solutions for retirement and financial future. Through a combination of creativity, strategic foresight, and attention to detail, she can ensure her clients receive plans and services that are specifically tailored to their current needs and future goals.

How she serves Educators, Police & Fire, and Faith-Based Organizations: Jefflyn is committed to helping clients within these industries implement, grow, and partake in the best possible outcomes for their financial future. She prides himself in her ability to listen to what her client's goals in life and finances are. She pairs listening and a direct ability to pay attention to the small details of each client's story. Those two characteristics allow for a client to feel heard and for Encore to become a major asset for her clients. Helping these professionals eliminate tax, losses, and fees is something that she takes pride in. It makes her smile to know her clients realize they can have financial freedom.

How she serves Small Business Owners: Jefflyn is able to customize a program that will fit her clients from all areas of life. She can strengthen your company by reducing employee turnover, attracting new hires, and retain key employees. With the understanding that not every company has the same goals and situation, and she is able to connect each employer with an array of financial solutions. Our customized services such as tax reduction, legacy planning, employee benefits, and business financial security are all tailored to each client and reflects an understanding that she is always looking out for her client's best interest.

Prior to her career in financial services, Jefflyn worked 5 years as a Financial Analysis for the County of San Bernardino, and 5 years for the Internal Revenue Service as a Collection Deputy. She has received a master's in business administration from Almeda University and a Bachelor of Science in Organizational Leadership from Azusa Pacific University. Additionally, Jefflyn has received certificates from the American College of Financial Services for Retirement Income Certification Planning (RICP) and The Institute of Business and Finance for Certified Annuity Specialization (CAS). She also has received a Doctorate in Ministry from Long Beach Bible College. She plays the piano, does a little bit of singing and is active in church work/community service.

If you have any questions about Encore, Jefflyn or our services, please contact me at the info below.

- Jefflyn Dangerfield
- Reginal Marketing Director
- Encore-FFS/NLG/ANICO/Columbus Life

Email: imyouragentpc@gmail.com
Telephone Number: 909-520-9868

Please subscribe, follow and like:

- Facebook: ImYourAgentPC
- Instagram: ImYourAgentPC
- YouTube Channel: I'm Your Agent PC
- Podcast: https://podcasts.apple.com/us/podcast/imyouragentpodcast/id1531948189

www.ingramcontent.com/pod-product-compliance
Lightning Source LLC
Chambersburg PA
CBHW070937080526
44589CB00013B/1544